AF176537

1

Hello, everybody,

my name is Christian and I am from Germany.

I have been writing texts since 2006. My categories are politics, society, criticism, against capitalism, career, value creation, dreams, goals, grief, suffering - defeats and victories... I even deal with temporary work and working models.

Up to now I have mainly written texts in German language. It is just easier for me to write in my mother tongue.

I listen to a lot of music, so bands from all over the world. Because I love to read and listen to English lyrics, I have now chosen the "language for the whole world" with this book.

I am a book author and write out of passion. I love to write for people, about

feelings, everything that makes us happy.
I write against terror, hate, fear, doubt, depression!

This book should be a sign - against the pressure of society.

Please excuse my bad english. Have mercy on me. LOL

Your Christian

Chapter one – POETRY ART –

1. Hell City
2. Life is a maze
3. Just a dream
4. Nightmare
5. Magic key
6. Sadness
7. Mental damage
8. Depressive grades
9. Fear of death
10. Lost books
11. My pain
12. There is another side
13. Bad riddle
14. Ruins
15. Chaos life
16. Against the pressure of society
17. Tell me why!?
18. High Society
19. One of a million
20. Feelings and awareness
21. This life

Hell City

The lights burn like a fire
Glowing red and hot
This town is like a cage he's hired!
It is the place from hell!

Demons fly to the dark sky
Crimson moon until dawn
Daybreak
It is like the darkness of night

The air is hot and sticky
Your lungs are filled with smog
There are monsters and hunters
Hellhounds and snakes, you are shocked!

The devil is celebrating
The evil dances
Hell City
Hell City

This city feeds on sorrow
The shadow eats him up
Everything that disappears
In the darkness, never reappears!

Life is a maze

Life is a maze
Between rats and maggots
It is a walk in the dark
You must take care of yourself!

The smell of society is toxic!
Evil reigns supreme!
Doom and damnation
A glorious game for the devil

Waste and decay
Death walks the streets
Lies and sins cry out for mercy!
The downfall begins

The sun has fallen from the sky
Hope lies in flames and ashes
Broken glass and pain are our signs
All made by our hand

Greed and might
Has brought disaster on us
Hellfire!
Angels of darkness rising up

It is a paradise of the dark
The fire is hot, like the devil's eye
There is no turning back
It is a shadow world

Just a dream

A thousand voices in your head
That bury your voice
All what you hear, is your silence
But you can still hear their noise

You lose yourself in thought
Far in the dark!
you run aimlessly through –
The mist in an endless park

You are looking for a way out
You want control
You are driven by pain
But you have hope in your soul

There is nothing
Emptiness fills life
If you could remove it
You would cut with a knife

Wake up! Wake up!
It is just a dream
Your life is your own
If you want it, you have to scream!

Nightmare

A nightmare awakens
When the soul rests
Evil reigns
When good sleeps

The darkness dances with joy
When the light goes out
Doom comes
It knows no mercy!

Shadow creatures
Are hunting you!
all night long!
They rejoice in your nightmare fear!

The devil has 1000 faces
He always has his eye on you!
He screams, he laughs, he plays
You can't outrun him!

When the night awakens
The sunlight dies.
The heart fills with darkness
The evil never sleeps

Magic key

My wish is to escape, to another world
Where freedom and health flourish
I want to be free
From constraints

A magic key
For a kingdom built on dreams
Love and peace -
Never miss a day there again

No place for fear and darkness
No tears and no worry
This kingdom is hope
Colours, elves and fairies

The pain is healed
Wounds are roses, they bloom
War and terror
Is here eternal peace and love

That wish is just -
A Neverland
That magic key
I'll never find it

Hard is –
The reality
I feel darkness and pain
Why do I believe in this magic key?

Sadness

Fear and darkness
Nice to see you, my friend
You never leave my side
Not even when I dream to the end

I've known you for so long
You're under my skin
The soul screams, but I remain silent
My chest is cracking

Is my life the beginning of death?

My breath is breaking
My heart is so very heavy
The pain is pressing
I feel only emptiness!

I'd like to feel joy again
The sadness likes my insides
I can't chase it away
It holds me for all time

Heartache
Pressure on the chest
Breathing is difficult
I can't breathe!

My mind is going round and round
My lungs are suffocating
Does death begin?
What is happening to me?

Mental damage

A twinge in my head
My nerves are at the limit
Neurological damage
They are traces of my life

I have lived in fear
I've always done my duty!
My psyche is destroyed
Mentally it is anything but beautiful!

It's not my fault!
I have to write these lines!
It is my impulse!
The soul speaks with these signs!

I need to write!
I can't live without writing!
This state of affairs is not a long-term
solution!
But the solution is to look for it!

Serious psychological damage
I'm not writing a joke here!
This is deadly serious.
What the hell am I supposed to do?

Depressive Grade

Negative flows
Interference
the nerve pathways are disturbed
Depressive grades

Society and pressure
I feel used!
Serve only the purpose
I am confused

Depressive episodes
I live in fear of death
Part of social phobia
How is my health?

Time goes by
Now while I'm sitting here.
Do I wait for my time?
I am already very near her

I'm breaking down here
My heart feels only pain
I've lasted this long
I can't go on!

I sink into tunnel vision
The way it is today, it's gonna last for the
rest of my fucking life!
I close my eyes.
Finish the life

Fear of death

Sometimes at night, I scare!
My heart is pumping
My heart pricks
Heartbeat very loud!

Nerves are thrilling endlessly
I am braced
I am cramped up
My pulse is trembling

I get no rest
No possibility to relax
Horror Life
For a long time I've felt this

Not to breathe a break
always under stress
It's my hell on earth
I no longer fear the devil

My life is pure hell
Pain and suffering
This is –
Well known to me

Lost books

I have so much on my shoulders
Everything I have to do in my life!
Where do I keep the secrets?
Memories that have no importance!

pictures of a past
I am someone else today
These pictures sometimes fly –
Like loose pages from a book I no longer
have!

Tell me, isn't it crazy?
How I once was and how I lived
Everything forgotten and lying on the
floor
Pages that are distributed throughout the
room!

The drawers stacked full
Notepad with the inscription -
IMPORTANT -
Today everything without meaning!
No content, totally correct!

Some things in life are like lost books
Are they books that have been sorted out
But memories come back
Many a time, back to the head

My Pain

That's life out there!
Where the sun shines
I sit in here and listen to the soul -
Cry out the pain!

I don't want to live
This life anymore!
I want a different –
Fucking life!

My heart is swimming in sadness
Feeling of 1000 knife-stabs inside me
No prospect of hope
Hopeless, everything as sharp as the knife
is!

Powerless and painful
That's how I feel on these days!
I wouldn't be writing here
Then I would die!

I walk through broken glass
Streets covered with dirt!
The situation seems hopeless!
In this sense, to the next days!

There is another side

This view is anything but good
I want to get out of here so bad!
I have to get out!
And I want to get out of here fast.

But there is another side
One chance and one possibility
Between hanging on and giving up!
I'm the one who keeps the balance!

The world is coming to an end
Is the sun coming up?
Well, either I save myself!
Or I lose control

there is another side
I must not lose faith
There's another way!
It pays to keep going on.

No looking back
Just look ahead!
The aim is up ahead
Look closely!

Bad Riddle

Life is strange
It doesn't feel real!
An evil tale, an evil riddle
I'm in the madness

Is it just a dream?
Is it reality?
It's bizarre and crazy
I'm going fucking crazy!

Who's holding me prisoner?
Who judges my thoughts?
It is a bad riddle
I am the players...

it's a chessboard
Black and white the tiled floor
I move like in a labyrinth
All passageways are locked!

No way out
I do not know the solution...
I only know one thing
I'm going mad

Everything has its roots
everything has its beginning
Everything comes to an end
Except this bad riddle!

Ruins

My soul is burned out
My bones are in ruins!
Everything looks okay from the outside!
But inside, it's really different

Everything is
Fragile and shaky
The framework in unstable
A few more failures, I can't take it!

Fires that can't be put out anymore!
I am the hearth in all the fire and heat
The area is under fire
Ashes and smoke draw the sky
The flames beat about wildly
Rescue is hopeless

The globe is on fire
My heart of darkness
Wherever I am
Too far from hope!
Powerless and tired
A defeated warrior
This is my face now
Only my ruins remain!

Chaos life

Hello, hello
My life is a chaos
Eyo, eyo
It's the dark side of glamour and gloss

My heart and my soul
My skin and my bones
My head is tired
Driven by loss and sorrow

My life it hurts me
My colour of life is black
With my broken wings
I won`t come back!

The victory is long lost
The defeat of my garb
All the colours that used to be
They' re wearing dark

The shame keeps running
The fool makes his game.
No matter what happens
He is to blame

Against the pressure of society

This one makes noise
Even if you can't hear a sound
These lines are like a -
Very strong bounce

This is about you and me
This is our life!
This is a heavy metal song-booklet
Everything we do will be wide spread

We all stand up together
Against the pressure of society
All that we are and all that we have been,
we never forget our humanity

Let's send a united signal.
People should live, not suffer!
With every knockdown,
Everything will be even tougher!

Capitalism and finances
They must never be commandments!
Faith, peace and freedom -
These are our statements!

Tell me why!?

Please tell me why –
This world has such a sad face
Why are there so many –
Grey and dark days?

Why does sadness feed my heart?
Why is sorrow my greatest part?
Why does everything seem so hopeless
Why do I have the feeling of loneliness?

In my world the sun cries
Every hope dies
This reality is my place
Damn! These are dark days!

What does the darkness like about me?
She locks me up, so she's free!
It's been that way my whole life
My head and my heart are strife

Who do I ask these questions to?
Why do I ask so many questions?
I never get answers!
Everything has no association!

High Society

Where are the superheroes?
Where are those who can still save the
world?
We're destroying ourselves in a pointless
contest!
Does anyone else speak the word of truth?

So many ways we destroy ourselves!
So many souls that are already crying!
What is happening to us humans?
The money is a holy dying!

Money is all that matters here
No matter how many tears the earth cries
The greed of man is so -
Like the shit heaps with a thousand flies!

Disease and decay
People are without food!
but the high society...
She celebrates parties really good!

One of a million

We live in a paradise of plastic
At the highest level of technology
Always better and higher and higher!
We'll be machines manipulated biology

Mental suffering is on the increase
The world in progress
More than one hundred percent!
Prototypes in test

Everything faster, everything better
Errors are not acceptable
Function at the push of a button
The result is profitable

No consideration for human losses
There are enough of us - 8 billion
So what does your life matter?
You're just one of a million...

Feelings and awareness

How do I explain my feelings and my consciousness?
Since childhood I have been suffering from anxiety.
Fear of loss, fear of failure, fear of death!
I grew up with fears and panic attacks.
Due to my bronchial asthma disease and the associated respiratory distress attacks, I had to get to know the fear of death very early in childhood!

Even at the age of 10 I almost suffocated.
An experience that was over 24 years ago, but still stuck in my head!
In 2012 another asthma attack!
Cortisone injections that widened my airways, since that time I also need a cortisone spray!

My feeling of life and consciousness -
Since childhood, school, training and my professional life, I have always held out!
Without a sound, without a murmur, without resisting all unpleasant things!

In all these years, until today - depressive feelings have accumulated, have literally collected in me and nourished me!

Today, I question myself - life, society - life and death. It is a strange feeling I have inside me, it is this crass and intense consciousness of having to die!
According to this, my thoughts rotate about sense and meaningfulness!
I want to live a little more before I have to die! And to do something meaningful in my life than to have to function all the time!

I am so close and clear to the consciousness of the offence why I think and feel the way I do!

Lifetime, health! Everything that always counts, at least ALL say so - THE WHOLE SOCIETY!

But what really counts:
Which car do you drive?
Which profession did you learn?
How much do you earn on the job?
Do you have a house?
Do you have a job?

Endless fucking questions but the most important of all questions, nobody asks them!

ARE YOU HAPPY?

In this sense, I will always, really always fight, write and draw attention to depressive moments, episodes and impressions!
It is time that society starts to rethink and act accordingly!

What person is still happy here in all the state in which we live every day?

I worry too much where others don't or only waste thoughts on power and money...

But I know, people who "tick like me" - who feel like that, I will and want to reach!

I am writing this for all those who want a healthy life at last!

This life

If this life -
Still worth living
Without electronics, without plastic
No cars, just pedestrian traffic!?

Would it be the same life for me without
listening to music and reading books?
Or would it be for me
Doesn't make any sense anymore?

I'm questioning this life here
Myself included, in everything I say.
We live and die
Fading and dying away with time
Tell me, because I wonder -
What will ever be left of us?!

Are we all just on a journey?
A small effect in the universe
Until everyone here has finished -
Everything begins and goes around!
Just a second
In the whole time frame
We come alone, we go alone
it all stays the same?

Chapter two – RAP ART –

1. World-shot-down
2. UCN1E
3. All or nothing
4. Lost and dust
5. Available
6. Time is running out
7. Hope is lost

World-shot-down

Shutdown, Lockdown
Shoot out, shotgun
World shoot down
Entry, exit, breakdown!

Politics, it is shit.
It's a really global hit!
Bad people want to govern...
We are neither a copy nor a cover

They paint the wall with our blood
Then the wave breaks and the flood.
Only enter their royal palaces
Never our neighbourhood

Holy good circle, they call themselves a
Supervisory committee...
They guide us, lead us, feed us
Make us sick, poor, worn out and destroy!

UCN1E Utd. Continents Nations 1st Elite

They rule and lubricate
Everything they do is so desolate.
News reports, people are not stupid!
Spread all over the world, it's their troops
We're on the field
But we are without a shield
It is the ground of death
Their brains all on meth!

They erase our lives
They all wear their stripes!
Your life is in their pull
Your breath goes out, wonderful
They play the heroes in the game!
They make mistakes, we are to blame
They get the medal when people are dying
They get respect, but they haven't tried
anything!

They care about themselves and their
money
Their notes make the day sunny
Children and sick people die!
This is the truth, the lies are mountain

All or nothing

People live in fear
Cause she's playing with us here
You must work, pay, every day
Groundhog Life, let us play

Working without thinking!
You must swim well when you are sinking.
Always wear boots
The shit stays with the roots

Evil never sleeps
No matter what it speaks.
it's unbreakable and has no leaks!
It is made of snakes and thieves

The devil has sharp teeth and
He has watchful eyes
He's hiding in the skies!
He doesn't know mercy, roll the dice!

Bad time, bad card
Life isn`t easy, die hard
Pain is there, sorrow is there
All or nothing, tomorrow is anywhere

Lost and dust

This is an alibi, of lost and dust
All just lies you don't trust!
It's steps of her boots
But they claim they're the roots!

They lead you down paths
But these are traces of the past
They embody their new face
You are the fool in their race!

False pride and false honour!
Look at all the crosses in the corner!
Fallen soldiers from their game
You're not a toy soldier, it'll never be the same!

Faces soaked in tears
You want those lines to disappear!
Erase borders for peace!
You see it pure and the only crease!

You want to make a difference,
You want them to say the war, it all ends!
This is against the pressure of society!

Available

In my work I am available!
but in my spare time I live!
Nobody discovers my talent
Then I'm sorry!

I'm just supposed to function all the time.
They always expect only from me!
They don't take the time to get to know me.
But that's not my problem

I have applied
They chose me.
Your expectations are high!
But nothing comes from them!

I've switched off.
Shutting down my system!
I'll boot it up after work!
I'm alive, I'm on the line!

I need completion
Give it to me and I'm good!
Don't give it to me.
then I'm just available!

Hope is lost

The time ist running out
I see the falling skies
The end is near
It's the last rolling dice

The hope is lost in fog and dust
The faith is broken
All the words between us
Already spoken

Grey days, pale face
Empty life so long like a raceway
Thoughts of sadness –
Nothing it's okay!

I am a prisoner of my mind
What I want it's not to find
Can't get out of my head, out of my mind
I've lost my way, I`ve lost my sign

Where is the light?
Nothing's gonna right!
No stars are shining bright!
Every day is like a hard fight!

Chapter three – LAST WORDS –

1. Lock and key
2. Lies
3. Your life
4. Entertainer
5. School rules
6. Don't close your eyes

Lock and key

They push you down
They're bringing you to your knees
You're their door lock
They turn the keys

You're just a part
In a rotating circle
You are the toy
they use you universally

Who do you want to talk to?
When everyone is just talking but not
hearing
The lies of the society
They infect us, they make us sick

They preach in the schools
Of social behaviour!
But politics is corrupt
Life lie! Fucking bullshit!

Lies

Keep a lookout at night
When everything is asleep
For the sleeper he does not sleep in the
night!
The truth weeps

The lies of the day, they blind us
We're supposed to believe what they say!
We have to believe what they show!
We walk and never stay!
They manipulate our minds
they want to find out everything about
us!

genetic manipulation
Lab tests, radioactive!
Contamination, reproduction
The state helps actively!

People should be kept stupid!
Let them be busy!
This is how their game works
Everything is so good!

Your life

it's your life
it's your way
You determine your value!

Society distinguishes between classes!
Rich and poor!
Alive and dead!

Downfall
Rise
Dark side
Light

Are the paths also hard
Is it also heavy
It's your life
So you should give it your all!

try everything
You have dreams and goals
Believe in her and in you!
Go off and follow them!

Entertainer

We need entertainment!
Where are the entertainers?
We'll fight and laugh!
we are watching celebrity containers!

They're giving us the show!
Anything important doesn't matter!
As long as the odds are right!
You can laugh, so pay up!

The world a huge circus
Politics is a theatre
Criminals rule!
Horror movies are a joke in comparison!

Everyone needs to be entertained!
Films, videos or tease
Lifelong, grandiose season
The world is a madhouse
They're holding us prisoner!

School rules

As a child you go to school
There are teachers and there are rules
when you get older...
...you'll find that the rules are often
broken!

in the society...
... is lied to, cheated on, it's all about
money!
Used, exploited
Life isn't as sweet as honey!

Life is bitter as a lemon!
You must bite, you have no choice!
Either you eat!
Or you die, heads or tails

It's the game of society!
Stuck in chains!
There's no escape!
You must play your game

Don't close your eyes

Do not close your eyes
Keep them open and look carefully!
Can you see the procedures?
Do you recognize their system?

Will you go or stay
Look or look away
Whatever you decide to do
You are part of the way!

Good and bad
War and Peace
You are part of the world
Don't keep quiet, say your word!

The author Christian Hofmann was born on 5 March 1986 and lives in Germany in the federal state of Hessen.
The city where he lives is the university town of Marburg.

The author began writing in 2006.
Poems, rhymes, lyrics.
Through music and selected bands the author found his way to poetry!

He likes to listen to Rap and Rock/Metal.

The messages are especially important to him. The author calls himself a social critic.

His aim is to reach people who share or understand his opinion. Also to show people who think they are in the minority. He likes to point out the opposite!

Best regards Christian Hofmann

to all readers
to all fans around the world!

Stay strong friends!

until soon…

Impressum

Bibliografische Information der Deutschen
Nationalbibliothek: Die Deutsche
Nationalbibliothek verzeichnet diese
Publikation in der Deutschen
Nationalbibliografie; detaillierte
bibliografische Daten sind im Internet über
dnb.dnb.de abrufbar.

© 2020 Christian Hofmann
Herstellung und Verlag: BoD – Books on
Demand, Norderstedt
ISBN: 978-3-7519-8906-0